'*The Little Book of Prayer Experim*⌐
workbook. It's warm, easy approa⌐
a treasured book to many ... I predict wᴏⁿⁱ ᵤ⌐
eared copies.'

The Revd Kate Bottley, the 'Gogglebox vicar'

'*The Little Book of Prayer Experiments* is a practical, playful,
soulful guidebook for anyone who yearns to know God's love.
I recommend this book for sceptics and believers, young and
old, groups and individuals. Miranda Threlfall-Holmes has not
only provided a resource on prayer, she has given us a variety
of ways to free the human heart.'

Mark Yaconelli, author of Disappointment,
Doubt and Other Spiritual Gifts

Praise for *The Teenage Prayer Experiment Notebook*:

'An honest, comprehensive guide to prayer for teenagers. One
of this book's many strengths is that it encourages readers to
explore for themselves ... Indeed, why restrict this book to just
teenagers – the ideas here may well enrich the prayer lives of
many adults and families too!'

Grace Thomas, ArtServe magazine

'I'm particularly impressed by the diverse range of options
available including practical, interactive, written, virtual, food,
physical activity, quiet and loud variations. I encourage you

to buy this book for the teenager in your life ... and then ask if you can read it with them!'

Barry Mason, *thegoodbookstall*

'It is brilliant, with such good ideas. Can't wait to try them out with Holiday Club and Messy Church!'

Alison Evans, St Gabriel's Church, Heaton

'Who knew praying could be so much fun?'

'Recharge' youth group, St Michael and
All Angels Church, Houghton-le-Spring

'The beauty of this book is that it does exactly what it says on the cover – it is experimental and totally non-didactic. It releases and encourages the participant to think and try things out for themselves. I thoroughly recommend this book for students in church groups, schools, clubs, your own children, grandchildren and godchildren, and adults who would welcome thinking more widely about how to pray.'

Sally Barnes, mother and grandmother

'Brilliantly creative way of helping teens (and adults!) explore praying. It recognizes that we all connect with God in different ways.'

The Revd Nicki Hobbs, Assistant Curate,
Peterborough Diocese

Miranda Threlfall-Holmes is Vicar of St Mary Magdalene, Belmont and St Laurence, Pittington. Before ordination she first worked in brand management and was then a historian, and she holds first-class degrees in history from Cambridge and theology from Durham, and a PhD in medieval monastic history. Her publications include *The Teenage Prayer Experiment Notebook*, written with her son Noah (SPCK, 2015), *The Essential History of Christianity* (SPCK, 2012), *Being a Chaplain* (SPCK, 2011), *Monks and Markets: Durham Cathedral Priory, 1460–1520* (OUP, 2005), poems, and articles in the church and popular press. She trained for ministry at Cranmer Hall, Durham, served her title at St Gabriel, Heaton in Newcastle diocese, and was Chaplain of University College Durham and Interim Principal of Ustinov College Durham before taking up her current post in 2012. She is a member of the Church of England's General Synod and has been Vice-Chair of Women and the Church (WATCH). She is married to Phil, a chemical engineer, and they have three children.

Follow Miranda on Twitter @MirandaTHolmes and join in the conversation about prayer and the ideas in this book @PrayerExpNotebk.

THE
LITTLE
BOOK
OF
PRAYER
EXPERIMENTS

MIRANDA THRELFALL-HOLMES

SPCK

First published in Great Britain in 2016

Society for Promoting Christian Knowledge
36 Causton Street
London SW1P 4ST
www.spck.org.uk

British Library Cataloguing-in-Publication Data
A catalogue record for this book is available from the British Library

ISBN 978-0-281-07568-3
eBook ISBN 978-0-281-07569-0

Designed and typeset by Penguin Boy Ltd (www.penguinboy.net)
First printed in Great Britain by Ashford Colour Press
Subsequently digitally printed in Great Britain

eBook by Graphicraft Limited, Hong Kong

Produced on paper from sustainable forests

CONTENTS

FOREWORD

As conversation is to human friendship, so is prayer to divine friendship with God. At different times and in different circumstances, the friendship might involve chatting over coffee, taking a walk together or just exchanging knowing looks across a crowded room. It doesn't always involve words, but sometimes requires them. Whatever form it takes, prayer is essential for living and breathing and engaging with God – not just politely but also honestly and passionately, ideally with every part of our being.

I commend this little book to help you to 'just do it'. It matters more *that* you do it than *how* you do it. Most people find praying a challenge – sometimes because they're stuck in a rut, other times because they can't find the words or haven't yet established a regular pattern. Either way, this book will likely provide some useful ideas, whether for refreshment or for routine.

FOREWORD

As I have occasionally said to a person claiming that God isn't there or doesn't exist: just try talking to him, lifting yourself and all your cares up ... and see what happens.

The Bible teaches that prayer is the most powerful transformational force in the lives of individuals, churches and even nations. History shows us that whenever and wherever people have turned to God in prayer, they have rediscovered their purpose and been renewed and empowered.

Jesus prayed fervently, sometimes declining food or sleep in order to have time with his heavenly Father. The disciples were so fascinated that they begged him, 'Lord, teach us how to pray'. If you ever echo the same longing, you will likely be as grateful for this book as I am.

Justin Welby
Archbishop of Canterbury

ACKNOWLEDGEMENTS

This book started life as a blog, 'The Teenage Prayer Experiment', in which I wrote an idea for prayer each week, and then my teenage son Noah tried it out and blogged about how he had found it. As the blog grew more popular, individuals and church youth groups around the country began to use the ideas. We then published the ideas, and plenty more, as *The Teenage Prayer Experiment Notebook* (SPCK, 2015), which also included many ideas and comments generously contributed by teenagers and youth group leaders around the country.

When *The Teenage Prayer Experiment Notebook* was published, I began to receive comments from people asking why it was labelled as being for teenagers, and suggesting it might be published again in an alternative version for adults. One person, on the team of a retreat house, wrote to me to say that she

ACKNOWLEDGEMENTS

had had to buy her daughter a second copy, because she was complaining at the number of times the book disappeared from her room to be used during retreats. Several vicars wrote to say that the simple, clear explanations of different prayer styles, and the encouragement to experiment, were exactly what they needed to give to adults in their congregations, but they worried that they might feel patronized if given a book for teenagers.

This book is the result, and I am very grateful to SPCK for catching the vision and agreeing so enthusiastically to publish this edition. I remain hugely grateful to my son Noah and all the others who contributed to and helped form the initial idea for this book, and to all those who have so enthusiastically championed it and shared it with others. Finally, thanks to Mina Munns for permission to use two of her Bible colouring sheets in this book.

HOW TO USE THIS BOOK

INTRODUCTION

This is not a book to teach you about prayer. It is a book to encourage you to try prayer out for yourself. Using it, you can try out many different types and methods of prayer that have been used by Christians in different times and places. You can find out which methods suit you and – just as importantly – which don't.

Maybe you are a new Christian, exploring confirmation or baptism, or just beginning to dip your toe into church? This book will give you some easy first steps to take in exploring what this prayer business is all about.

Many people like to describe themselves as 'spiritual but not religious'. If that is you, then this book will help you explore what your own spirituality might be, and give you some old and new paths to follow.

Or you might be a lifelong Christian who is looking to broaden and deepen your prayer life. This book will introduce you to many of the riches of the Christian spiritual tradition, and help you to encounter them for yourself.

My own spiritual journey has led me to believe that becoming a Christian is not primarily something you can learn about academically, it is something you have to experience from the inside. The way to encounter God and to find out about praying is by giving it a try – 'taste, and see that the Lord is good', as the Bible puts it. And I believe that the living God always wants to encounter us, and is just waiting for us to make any move – however small – in God's direction. Are you up for it? Then let's get experimenting! Give the ideas a try, and see what happens.

Each experiment has three parts:

1 A brief introduction to the prayer idea being suggested. This explains why and how that particular method has been used in the Christian spiritual tradition.

2 The experiment itself: what to do, any equipment you will need, where to do it.

3 Space for your own notes on what using that prayer idea was like: what happened, how did it make you feel, would you do anything differently if you were repeating the experiment?

USING THIS BOOK ON YOUR OWN

You don't have to read the book from start to finish, or try the experiments in any particular order, or even try all of the experiments. I have arranged them so that different styles of prayer are mixed up: if you start at page one and go through to the end, you will find that an active or creative prayer idea is usually followed by a more reflective one, and so on. But you can choose to do them in any order, or just pick out the ones that sound most interesting to you.

The book includes space for you to make notes on how you found each experiment, and also for you to note down any ideas you have had about how you

might do things differently next time. For some
of the more craft-based experiments, there is a
'doodling' alternative: you can make the thing
suggested, but if that is impractical for any
reason, or simply if you prefer, then you can write,
draw and doodle on the paper version that is
included.

There will be experiments that you love, some no
doubt that leave you cold, and others you feel
lukewarm about. You can only know which are which
by trying them out!

USING THIS BOOK ON A RETREAT

If you have brought this book with you on a retreat
or quiet day – or are picking it up from the bookstall –
then you have time to try out several of the ideas
included here. You can use the book both as a retreat
or quiet day resource and as a prayer journal to record
what happens during your retreat.

I suggest that you begin with either the breathing
meditation (p. 21) or the colouring (p. 1), and ask God

to help you use this first activity to calm yourself, and to enter God's presence at this time.

Then, depending on the time you have available, try a variety of the other activities. For example, how about using the ACTS (Adoration, Confession, Thanksgiving, Supplication) structure (pp. 39–77)? If your retreat house has a full-size labyrinth, then do take the opportunity to walk it (p. 117). Or try a prayer walk (p. 11) around the locality – this will be a very different experience depending on where you are.

If you have a private room, then you could take the opportunity to try praying in different bodily positions (p. 95).

Finish your day with the Examen (p. 135).

As you use the book, do make the time to write up your thoughts, feelings and reflections in the notebook pages – and feel free to scribble, doodle and journal in the margins and on the text too, if you wish! You could use the blank pages on the insides of the cover to note down any thoughts, resolutions or reflections that have emerged during the retreat.

USING THIS BOOK IN A GROUP

You may want to use the book in your prayer group or cell group, or as a church prayer experiment project. Each person taking part will ideally need his or her own copy of the book to make notes in before sharing them with the group.

You can organize a prayer experiment group in various different ways:

1 'BOOK GROUP' STYLE

If the members of your group are fairly organized, and usually the same people come every time, then you can set an experiment as 'homework' between sessions. Each group member can try that type of prayer out before you meet again, and make their notes in the notebook pages. Then, when you meet up as a group, share your notes and discuss your experiences.

For: Everyone gets to try the experiment in private, and your notes aren't influenced by what others say. You will also have more time for discussion in the group.

Against: It won't work if people don't actually do their homework. If one person hasn't managed it one week, you can cope, but if you regularly have more than one person who can't contribute to the discussion because they haven't tried out the experiment on their own, then your meetings will be frustrating and less effective.

2 'PRAYER GROUP' STYLE

Alternatively, you could choose one experiment for each meeting and actually do it as part of the group meeting. This works particularly well with the craft-based experiments, for which someone needs to have got the bits and pieces together first. If you do this, then you will need to decide at the end of each meeting what you will be doing next time, and who will be responsible for gathering together any resources that will be needed.

HOW TO USE THIS BOOK

At the beginning of the meeting someone can read out the introduction to the experiment, before the same person or someone else reads out the instructions for the experiment. Everyone then does the experiment – preferably without discussion, either in silence or with soft music playing in the background. Someone will need to be responsible for timekeeping, and give people a five-minute warning to end their prayer time and fill in their notes. Then come together again as a group to share your notes and discuss your experiences.

For: Needs no preparation for most people, and it doesn't matter if people miss a week. Just one person needs to be responsible for gathering together any resources.

Against: Space might be an issue. For some of the more contemplative experiments, members of the group might want to sit somewhere privately: do you have enough nooks and crannies or quiet corners for them to disperse to? People will need to be disciplined about not chatting during the prayer time, which can be tricky when it is a craft activity – the leader will need to be confident in enforcing this discipline so that everyone can actually experience the activity as a time of prayer.

3 'WORKSHOP' STYLE

If you want to give people a taster of lots of different prayer ideas in one go, or if you would rather hold a day or morning workshop than have a regular meeting, many of these experiments work well as the material for a prayer workshop. Your planning team will need to choose a selection of experiments from the book, ideally a mix of active and contemplative ideas. You can hold the workshop in a parish hall or community room, in a church, in a school, or even at home: just choose the number of experiments that you have space for. They can be laid out around one big hall, or in the various nooks and crannies of a church, or in different rooms, depending on the space you have available. I have held events like this in churches, church halls, libraries, and even in the hallway of a university building at a clergy conference! For each experiment that you choose you will need, at the minimum, a table and some chairs around it.

I suggest that you begin by gathering everyone together and giving a brief introduction to the session. Explain that different prayer experiments can be found on each table, and that the participants can go around them in whatever order they like. They can spend as long or as short a time at each one as they wish – I have often found that some people will spend the whole time at one table, while others will try out all the experiments in turn.

On each table you will need to have at least one copy of this book, with the relevant pages marked with a bookmark or (preferably) a sticky note. If you are expecting lots of people it would be a good idea to have more than one copy on each table, and/or to also write out some simplified versions of the instructions so that queues don't develop as people wait to read the instructions. Alternatively, you could have somebody stationed at each table to introduce the activity – this is especially useful if some participants find reading difficult.

I have found that a good combination of activities is:

- Labyrinth (p. 117);
- Praying with beads (p. 105);
- Colouring sheets (p. 1);
- Confession stones (p. 49);
- Thanksgiving jar (p. 59).

And, if you can possibly manage it, build a prayer den (p. 31) in the space, especially if you are doing this in a large hall. You could also add in a group prayer walk (p. 11), or have maps with suggested prayer walk routes available for people to do on their own. If it is not a drop-in session but you know people will be there for the whole time, you could end the day by leading everyone in a silent breathing meditation (p. 21) or the Examen (p. 135).

For: You can introduce a large number of people to a variety of prayer ideas in one session. There is no long-term commitment to join a regular group. You could combine this with an existing cell group structure by holding a workshop for everyone together, and then discussing it in the next meetings of your individual cell groups.

Against: You will need to find a suitable space and advertise the session well in advance. The organizers will need to gather a wide range of resources together and do quite a bit of setting up and clearing away on the day. You probably won't know how many people will turn up until the session starts, so setting up the stations needs some guesswork and willingness to over-cater.

AND FINALLY . . .

However you use this book, the most important thing is that you actually try the experiments out. The only way to tell what praying in a particular way is like is to try it. It is no good just reading about it. Even if you want to read the book through before starting, do then choose one experiment, put the book down, and give it a try.

Enjoy experimenting!

EXPERIMENT #1

COLOURING THE BIBLE

LETTING THE BIBLE SPEAK TO YOU

One of the oldest forms of prayer in the Christian tradition is reading the Bible. That might not sound much like prayer to you, as nowadays we often think of prayer simply as being what we do when we are sitting quietly with our eyes closed, asking God for things. You might be more used to thinking of the Bible as something you read for information, or instruction. But reading the Bible prayerfully is a very important strand of the Christian spiritual tradition.

One way that Christians use the Bible in prayer is to focus on a short passage, staying with it for quite a long time. Sometimes people say that when they read a Bible passage once, or even twice, it stays as just words on a page. But when you've read it three, four or five times, suddenly something about it might jump out at you, or you might hear it differently.

This is what people mean when they say the Bible has 'spoken' to them: suddenly a word, or a phrase, has jumped out at them and seems to mean something specific for them. Or they suddenly notice something different about a story they have heard many times before, and understand something new about it. You might find you suddenly see a similarity between something that happens in the passage and what's going on in your own life, or feel that one particular word or phrase is what God wants to say to you just at this moment. This doesn't always happen dramatically, but if you read and meditate on a passage several times and stay with it long enough, you will almost always find that something about it seems new to you by the end.

There has recently been a surge of popularity in 'mindfulness' colouring books for adults. Millions of people have found that there is something relaxing, calming and meditative about spending a long period of time concentrating on something beautiful, and enjoying colours and shapes for their own sake. One way that medieval monks often spent time meditating on the Bible was by copying it out and decorating it. Illuminated manuscripts often had large decorated letters and elaborate borders, and the text itself was beautifully and painstakingly written, sometimes with certain words or letters picked out in different colours.

THE EXPERIMENT

Colouring in or writing out a Bible passage can give you all the benefits of mindful colouring, and the process also means that you spend a good long time with a particular phrase or passage, giving it the chance to speak to you. I've included a couple of illustrations in the book that you could use, but various books and printout sheets of suitable illustrations are available.

The Lindisfarne Scriptorium produces some lovely books of very intricate designs based on Bible passages and Celtic prayers (these are available to purchase online at <www.lindisfarne-scriptorium.co.uk>). There are also several individual sheets available free online, for example at the Flame Creative website (<www.flamecreativekids. blogspot.co.uk>, under 'Colour in prayers'). Just find one you like and print it out, or use the two provided here, which are reproduced by kind permission of Flame Creative.

Or you could make your own. Choose a passage from the Bible that is just a sentence or two long – you could ask someone else to suggest one for you, or you might remember a story that has stuck in your mind, or

4

you can find one by just flicking through the Bible. Take a sheet of paper (A4 is fine, A3 even better) and fill it with the words. Try to think not so much of 'writing it out' but of drawing each letter or word. Enjoy deciding the best way to lay the words out on the page, what style of writing fits the passage best, how you might illustrate it. It will probably work best if you make the writing, or at least some of the letters, hollow (like bubble writing), so that you can first draw the outlines of the words and then colour them in. That way you will spend longer with each word, rather than just quickly writing out the passage and spending the time decorating round the edge of it. Use the whole page, decorate every centimetre; make it as beautiful or dramatic as you can. Make the words the stars of the show. Alternatively, you could combine the process of writing out the Bible passage with a design from a mindfulness colouring book, by adding the words of the passage to the design, as part of your colouring of it.

Whatever you choose, you will be focusing on the words and images for quite a long time But the fact that your attention is occupied with the process of

drawing and colouring means you won't be too focused on the words themselves and the sort of things that you usually hear about them, or think you are 'supposed' to think. Your conscious mind will be occupied with the drawing and colouring, leaving your subconscious to meditate on the passage and allowing it to sink into you.

Approach this activity deliberately as a prayer, not just as decoration, and expect the words to become part of you and speak to you. Set plenty of time aside to do this, at least half an hour, ideally uninterrupted.

WHEN I TRIED THIS EXPERIMENT I FOUND . . .

SPENDING TIME WITH THESE WORDS . . .

THE THING I FOUND MOST VALUABLE WAS . . .

THINGS I WOULD TRY CHANGING NEXT TIME:

EXPERIMENT #2
PRAYER
WALKING

PRAYER WALKING

Prayer walking is a way of praying for a particular area when we might not know exactly what the people who live there need, or even who they are. It combines two ancient traditions of prayer: *intercession* and *pilgrimage*.

The first thing that might come to mind when you think about prayer is praying for God to help other people. This is called 'intercession', asking God to act on behalf of people or situations which we believe need God's help.

But we can often feel overwhelmed and confused by how much there is to pray for. And sometimes we don't know what is needed, so it is hard to know how to put it into words. This can be especially tricky when we want to pray for a specific area, perhaps the area in which we live, or in which our church is located, or an area which has had a lot of problems recently. We won't always know who all the people are that we are praying for, and the problems the area has may be very complicated.

Meanwhile, as in the second ancient tradition entailed in prayer walking – that of pilgrimage – the very fact of walking means that we are 'walking the walk not just talking the talk'. Pilgrimage involves physically taking a journey to a particular place of spiritual significance. The point wasn't simply to go to the place, it was to dedicate a period of time to God by making that journey. Traditionally, pilgrimages were undertaken on foot, so that there was considerable time and effort involved.

In prayer walking, we aren't just saying prayers, we are physically expressing our care for the place we are praying for, by walking around it. We are putting ourselves to some effort, not just sitting comfortably at home. And the action of walking occupies part of our conscious mind, so that prayer can flow more freely without us worrying too much about the exact words we use.

The main difference between prayer walking and going on a pilgrimage is that in prayer walking you don't need to have a particular destination in mind. Instead of walking to get somewhere, in this kind of prayer the walk itself, up and down the local streets, around the park or the shops, is the point. You could of course choose to walk to a particular place, maybe a viewpoint or church, but the point of this exercise is not to get there, but to pray for the places you pass through and think about on the way.

THE EXPERIMENT

Simply go for a walk! At first, start from your house and pray for the surrounding area. Or, if that isn't safe or appropriate for some reason, go to whatever place you would like to pray for. It is a good idea to make sure someone knows where you are going, of course.

As you walk, pray – not out loud, just in your head – for the places you pass. You might ask God to bless the people who live in the houses you walk past. If you pass a school, or shops, or offices, you could pray for the people who work there, and for all that they do. A particular business might make you think of specific things to pray for: a supermarket might spark off a thought about fair trade, or struggling farmers, or those who can't afford to eat properly. A newsagent might make you think about people in the news, or

14

about people reading their papers at home and what they are worrying about. A florist might remind you to pray for people who will be buying flowers this week to celebrate, or to mourn.

If you pass a church or other place of worship, pray for the people who meet there. Depending on your local situation you might also want to pray for particular community tensions, or church projects.

Just let thoughts arise in your mind, and when you notice that you are thinking about something, pray for it.

There will probably be people passing you, on foot, in cars, on a bicycle or the bus. You might pray for God's Holy Spirit to fill the woman walking her dog, or for the man leaving the shop across the road to be aware of God's presence with him as he goes. If an ambulance goes past, pray for the paramedics and whoever they are on their way to help. A delivery van might make you think of praying for anyone whose birthday it is today, or for those who are lonely and never get letters or parcels.

As you return home, ask God to bless the whole area, and to show you how you can be a blessing to it. You might like to end by praying for your own home as you enter it.

A GROUP WALK

A variation you might like to try is to do this as a group, setting off from your church in twos or threes in different directions and meeting up back at church afterwards to share your thoughts and experiences, and to pray together for the whole area.

A 'SITTING' WALK

Another variation, particularly suitable if you or members of your group have mobility difficulties, is to pray for an area by 'taking a walk' around a map of it. Trace the roads and paths with your finger or a pen, praying for them as you go. You could even do this as a group activity in church, using a greatly enlarged map and giving everyone a marker pen or highlighter to pray with.

WHEN I TRIED THIS EXPERIMENT . . .

THE THING I ENJOYED MOST WAS . . .

THE TIME I FELT MOST UNCOMFORTABLE WAS . . .

ONE THING I PARTICULARLY NOTICED WAS . . .

THINGS I WOULD TRY CHANGING NEXT TIME:

EXPERIMENT #3
BREATHING
MEDITATION

ON?

etting time aside to be calm and
ferent from most other types of
that it is not about talking to God, or even
listening to God, but simply about being. The idea is
simply to sit there and let your mind be free from
thinking about anything in particular. You are not trying
to achieve anything, or say anything, or do anything:
you are just taking time to be.

In the Christian tradition, this process tends to be
called contemplative prayer rather than meditation, but
the technique or discipline is very similar. In Christian
contemplation, the underlying assumption is that when
you spend time just being, you are being with God. You
don't even have to busy yourself thinking about God:
just be, and maybe let yourself become aware of
yourself in God's presence.

MEDITATIVE TECHNIQUES

When you try it, you may well find that it is surprisingly
hard to simply sit still in silence, even for a few minutes.

Because people tend to find it very difficult, various different practices have developed to help you focus. The two main ones are concentrating on your breathing, and repeating the same word or phrase over and over – usually either in silence, or just under your breath. These are well-known techniques in virtually every spiritual tradition. They are often combined, so that you say a word, or part of a phrase, on the in breath, and repeat it, or say the other part of the phrase, on the out breath.

The actual word or phrase (known as a 'mantra' in some spiritual traditions) isn't important. Saying it isn't the point of the exercise; it is simply there to help you meditate (and it certainly doesn't have any sort of magical power). The phrase used most commonly in the Christian tradition is a very old, short prayer known as the Jesus Prayer: 'Jesus Christ, Son of God, Have mercy on me, A sinner'. This is normally used over four breaths: 'Jesus Christ' as you breathe in, 'Son of God' as you breathe out, 'Have mercy on me' as you take another breath in, and finally 'A sinner' on the second breath out. That four-breath pattern is then repeated over and over again. Other people use a favourite Bible verse, or simply the word 'God' or 'Jesus'. Don't worry about choosing the 'right' word. For now, I suggest that if you want to use words, you use the Jesus Prayer.

Some people also find visualization helpful. You can begin your meditation by imagining going into a secluded, beautiful place – somewhere you are alone and safe, and can leave whenever you want. It is often particularly helpful to imagine yourself walking into that place across a particular threshold: going through a gateway or door, or down some steps, and then sitting there. For example, you could imagine walking down some steps into a sunken garden, or through a gate into a meadow, or along a path through sand dunes to a secluded beach.

HOW IT WORKS

Physically, concentrating on your breathing calms you down and makes you more aware of your body. Mentally, it helps you to free your mind from distractions, and it gives you something to focus on while you deliberately take time out of your busy life.

Spiritually, it helps you to focus on who you really are in relation to God. All the things that you do and say to try to give a good impression to other people are stripped away. It also gives you space to listen to God: but don't let 'trying to hear God' become the point of the exercise! The aim is simply to be: don't expect any particular results.

THE EXPERIMENT

First, find somewhere you can be comfortable, still and undisturbed. Most people sit, but you should find the position that is most comfortable for you.

Next, it can help to set an alarm (on your phone, or a kitchen timer) for the amount of time you are going to put aside. This means that you don't have to keep opening your eyes to check the clock! I suggest that you start with 10 minutes – you may want to build up to 20 minutes or half an hour over time.

Then shut your eyes, and begin to concentrate on your breathing. Be aware of each breath in, and each breath out. If you are saying the Jesus Prayer, say a phrase on each breath, in and out. You will probably find that your breathing begins to slow down.

After a while, become conscious of your body: of the weight of your limbs, how it feels to be sitting. You might find that you begin to feel uncomfortable or self-conscious. You might also find yourself disturbed by noises from outside your room. Just notice what you are feeling or hearing. Notice it kindly, don't tell yourself off for being distracted by it. Mentally acknowledge what is there, then focus on your breathing again.

It is completely normal to find that all sorts of thoughts and worries come rushing in – from big important things that you must remember to do, to all sorts of trivialities. It is also normal to find that you suddenly realize your mind has wandered. Again, don't worry. When you notice a thought, a worry or a feeling, or realize that your mind has wandered, just notice it kindly, and then consciously return your focus to your breathing. If you find yourself panicking that you will forget something important, you might like to keep a notepad and pen by your side so that you can note things down, taking them out of your head and onto the page. It is when you are distracted by thoughts or worries that repeating something like the Jesus Prayer can be particularly helpful, as it gives you something specific to focus on.

Doing this might feel very odd. We are very rarely still and silent, with nothing to keep our minds occupied. So when we are, it can feel very uncomfortable. Even those who make a habit of meditating for half an hour or more a day find it difficult at times. You may find yourself getting very annoyed. Just accept any discomfort, notice it, and keep concentrating on your breathing.

If you are using the Jesus Prayer, you may want to drop a word or two at a time as you go, so that it gets shorter. In the end, you may be left with only one or two words, repeating those on the in and out breaths.

Keep at it until your alarm sounds. If you visualized going to a special place, now visualize leaving it: walk back out across that threshold, knowing you can return whenever you want. If you were using the Jesus Prayer, say it one last time and then say 'Amen', out loud.

WHEN I TRIED THIS EXPERIMENT I FOUND . . .

AT THE BEGINNING, BEING STILL MADE ME FEEL . . .

ONE THING I PARTICULARLY NOTICED WAS . . .

AS TIME WENT ON, I . . .

THE THING I FOUND MOST VALUABLE WAS . . .

THINGS I WOULD TRY CHANGING NEXT TIME:

EXPERIMENT #4

PRAYER DEN

A PLACE FOR PRAYING

Many people find it easier to pray in church, or in a chapel, than at home. There seems to be something helpful, when we want to pray, about deliberately going to a place that is set aside for prayer. In the past, wealthy Christians with grand houses would often have in their home a chapel, or a small room that was set aside for reading the Bible and praying. As well as the convenience of having somewhere at home, however, there is also a difference between praying in a big, public building and in a small, private space.

Praying in a big space has the advantage of making you feel part of something bigger than yourself. Huge, soaring ceilings are designed to lift your eyes and mind to God's majesty, and make you feel very small in comparison. And praying in a public building makes the important point that we are not only individual Christians, but part of the worldwide Church of Christ.

On the other hand, a small space of your own can feel much safer and more intimate. It can allow you to feel private with God, enable you to feel safe to be yourself without having to worry about what other people might be thinking of you. It can be a place where it feels that God comes to meet you, rather than you having to go to meet God.

Few of us have space for a chapel in our homes, but it's possible to make a prayer corner in almost any room. As you go through this book trying the various experiments, why not keep some of the things you make and put them together on a shelf or windowsill somewhere in your house that you pass regularly? By doing so you will build up your own personal collection of prayer objects and reminders, and create a prayerful space of your own.

THE EXPERIMENT

This experiment takes the idea of a prayerful space a step further. The aim is to make a prayer den, a small enclosed space to pray in – just big enough for one.

First, you'll need to decide where to build the den. Could you make it in the corner of your bedroom? Or maybe in a spare room, shed or garage? If it is summer, you might even create one outdoors. It could stay up for just an afternoon, or it could be semi-permanent, whatever suits the space you have available.

The easiest way to build your den is to pitch a tent. Pop-up 'festival' tents can be found quite cheaply in many bargain shops, or you could even use a child's play tent if you have one around. If you use one of these indoors you don't need to use any pegs or ropes, just sit it on the floor – and it can be 'pitched' and folded away in a matter of seconds. Other ideas that people have found work for them are a garden shed or summer house, a large walk-in cupboard, or

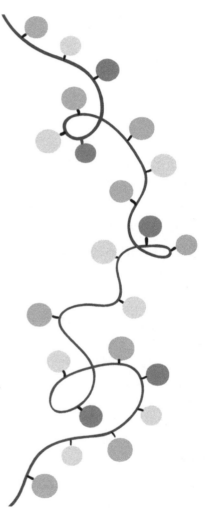

a folding clothes airer; or you could rearrange items of furniture (chests of drawers, chairs, etc.) to create a hidden corner. If necessary, cover your chosen framework with sheets, blankets, duvets and so on, to make a completely enclosed space. You want it to be comfortable to sit in for a reasonable length of time, so cover the floor with pillows, cushions or beanbags, or bring in a chair.

Now decide how to decorate the inside of your den. Think first about lighting. People who have tried this have particularly liked using fairy lights or battery-operated candles. Be careful only to use a low wattage lamp that doesn't get hot, to avoid any risk of fire.

What about pictures? You could add posters, postcards, or images of people or situations that you want to pray for. You could bring in a newspaper to pray through. And how about a journal, notebook and pen, or sketchbook? Maybe you would like to add items from your prayer corner, bunting or a rug. Make a space that feels snug and secure, somewhere you will enjoy sitting in and that feels very personal to you. Making the den can itself be a prayerful activity, as you think about what will help you to pray and look forward to being with God in the space you are creating.

Once you have built the den, it is time to start using it to pray in. Just go in, sit down, and imagine that God is in there with you. You can simply sit quietly, imagining yourself in God's presence, or talk with God, or say prayers that you know, such as the Lord's Prayer. Or why not try combining this experiment with others, and doing one or two of the other prayer activities suggested here in your den?

WHEN I TRIED THIS EXPERIMENT I FOUND . . .

AS I MADE MY OWN PRAYER DEN . . .

PRAYING IN THIS SPACE MADE ME FEEL . . .

THE THING I FOUND MOST VALUABLE WAS . . .

THINGS I WOULD TRY CHANGING NEXT TIME:

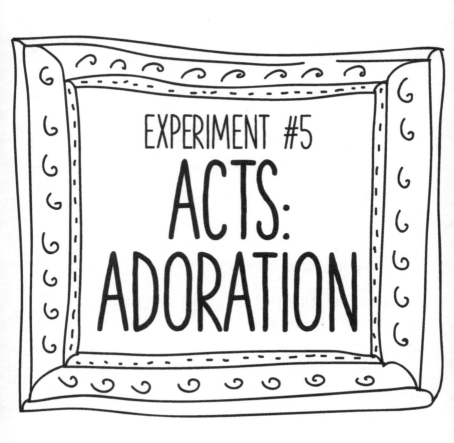

THE FOUR FOOD GROUPS OF PRAYER

There is a well-known formula for a balanced prayer life. It is known as ACTS, which stands for

1 Adoration (adoring God, standing in awe of God, praising God)

2 Confession (admitting all the ways we are not perfect, and resolving to do better)

3 Thanks (saying thank you to God for all that we have and are)

4 Supplication (asking God for things we need, asking for help for ourselves or others).

The idea is that a balanced prayer life consists of all four elements. Many people find that they actually do mainly number 4, with not very much of 1, 2 or 3. But think of them as being a bit like the food groups – proteins, carbohydrates, fats, etc. – which when eaten in the right combination make up a balanced diet. A balanced diet of prayer will include all the different elements, in a healthy combination.

The next four experiments each focus on one of these elements. Often, you will want to make sure you do all four each time you pray. But for now, we will look at each one individually.

ACTS 1: ADORATION

Adoration is thinking about, contemplating, how wonderful God is. It's rather like looking at a beautiful view, or enjoying eating something delicious: you're not so much talking or thinking about how great the thing is, you are just enjoying it and being aware of how special it is.

What reminds you how amazing God is? For some people, it might be being at the top of a high mountain, or seeing a beautiful sunset, or the ocean waves, or a huge storm. You might find yourself filled with a sense of awe at wild animals, or tiny insects, or vast crowds of people. Maybe for you, seeing aerial photographs of the world, a nature documentary, or hearing children play makes your heart soar.

Some people find their heart lifted and their mind turned to God's beauty, majesty and love by nature, while others find that human creativity or love or generosity is what fills them with wonder. So you might be moved to adore God by art, or by beautiful churches; by a soaring cathedral spire; by music of whatever kind; or by stories from charities who are working to relieve hunger, poverty and suffering.

Reminders of God's story in the Bible might also have this effect: from pictures on Christmas cards of the birth of Jesus to statues or stained glass pictures of the crucifixion, or the empty tomb, or stories from the Bible. Hearing certain Bible stories, or worshipping in church with family and friends, or singing certain songs, might also move you to a sense of adoring God.

THE EXPERIMENT

One way of expressing your wonder at God and God's world is to make an adoration collage. First, spend some time thinking about what moves you to a sense of awe and wonder. Maybe jot down a few notes on a sheet of paper.

Then, think about pictures that will illustrate those things for you. They might be literal depictions – a mountain, a sunset – or they might be more abstract. For example, if you have written 'peace' you might want to illustrate this by finding pictures of a dove, or of decommissioned weapons, or of a spa.

There are two ways of making an adoration collage. To make an actual collage that you can put up on the wall, search for the pictures you need in old magazines, newspapers and catalogues. You could also print out images you have found online. If appropriate, you might like to include words or phrases too.

Alternatively, you could make the whole collage electronically, searching for the images you want and making a digital collage or slideshow.

When you come to put the collage together, write 'I adore you, God, for . . .' or simply 'Adoration' in the middle, and surround the words with images that each make you feel awe, wonder or love for God and for all that God has made and done.

Finally, stick it up on the wall (having printed it out, if you have made it on the computer) so that it is a reminder for you of how amazing God is.

DOODLE VERSION

If you are away from home or don't have suitable materials to hand, then try using the doodle spaces provided on pages 43 and 48. As before, spend time thinking about what moves you to a sense of awe and adoration; and as you do so, doodle words, symbols or sketches in each frame.

WHEN I TRIED THIS EXPERIMENT I FOUND . . .

MAKING THE COLLAGE MADE ME FEEL . . .

AS I LOOK AT MY COLLAGE . . .

THE THING I FOUND MOST VALUABLE ABOUT
THIS WAS . . .

THINGS I WOULD TRY CHANGING NEXT TIME:

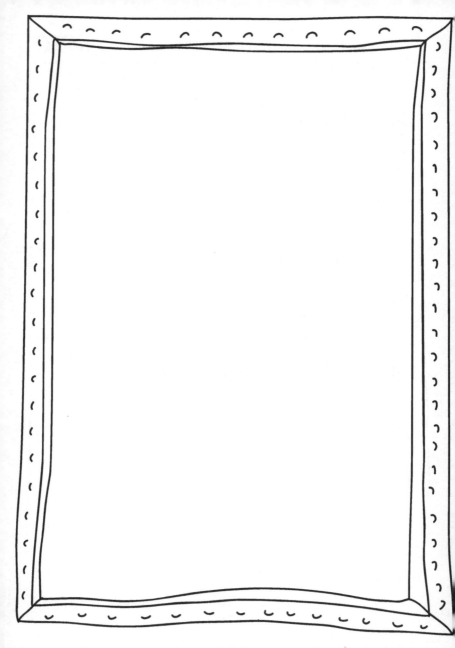

EXPERIMENT #6
ACTS:
CONFESSION

THE TWO MEANINGS OF CONFESSION

'Confession' has two distinct meanings in Christianity.

The first is the one you are probably more familiar with – owning up to what you've done wrong. Normally, this includes saying sorry and promising to try not to do it again – though we all know that is a promise we often don't keep! Most church services include a 'confession'. This is a time when the whole congregation says sorry to God for failing to reach the standard of human living that the Bible and Jesus' life set out for us.

The second meaning is again 'owning up', but this time to our faith. This kind of confession means standing up for what we believe in. In many churches we literally stand up for what we believe in, as everyone stands in the church service to say a creed (from the Latin word *credo*, meaning 'I believe') or other statement of faith: a short summary of what the Church believes about God.

Confession is the second element of the ACTS pattern of prayer. In our personal prayers, the very fact that

50

we are praying at all is a 'confession' of sorts. By the act of praying, we are 'confessing' – saying that we believe – that there is a God who hears and answers prayers. So in our personal prayers we don't very often say a formal 'statement of faith'. But for as long as people have been praying, owning up to what we've done wrong has been an important part of prayer.

CONFESSING: CHANGING THE FUTURE, NOT THE PAST

God, of course, already knows everything that we have done. So by confessing, we aren't letting God into a secret that we could otherwise keep to ourselves. But by confessing, we are forced to confront our own behaviour.

If we don't own up to what we are doing wrong, we can't change it. For Christians, the key idea is 'repentance', which is not just about confessing our mistakes, but actively committing to turning away from them and living differently. If we think, or try to pretend, that there is nothing at all wrong with how we are living our lives, then we are saying we don't intend to change. Sometimes we don't want to own up to things that are wrong because we are ashamed or embarrassed. We can be 'in denial' about our own behaviour as well as other people's: pretending to ourselves that everything is fine because we find something too painful to confront. But if we make a practice of regularly admitting that everything isn't perfect, we can help ourselves to focus on what changes we'd like to see.

Even for those who wouldn't call themselves Christian, admitting where things are going wrong and committing yourself to changing is a really important part of life. For example, athletes don't reach the top of their game by deciding they are so good there is nothing they need to work on. Musicians never become brilliant at their instrument by deciding that since they are already the best in the orchestra there is no need to practise.

It is important, when you confess as part of your private prayers, to remember that confession and God's forgiveness go together. One of the things that

Christians believe about Jesus' death on the cross is that as he died, he took on himself any blame and guilt that we should have for anything we might do wrong. So Jesus' death guarantees that God has already forgiven us. We don't confess because God won't like us otherwise: God always loves us, whatever we have done.

(A health warning: Sometimes people find this hard to believe, and can get stuck at feeling guilty. If this happens to you, or you can't shake off a feeling that God didn't mean to forgive you, then please go and talk about it to someone you trust from church, perhaps your vicar or a wise friend.)

THE EXPERIMENT

Find some stones (they don't need to be anything special, just collect them from your garden – or you can buy washed stones from many garden centres or home décor shops). Have at least three, and up to six or seven. Set a bowl of water in front of you, and put the stones in a pile.

Sit down and pick up the first stone. As you hold it, think about one thing in your life that is not as good as it could be. Own up to it. Then put the stone in the water: you are giving it to God, not holding its weight any longer. And it is being washed clean.

Pick up the next stone and think of something else in your life that is less than perfect, repeating the process as many times as seems right. When you have finished, you might like to end by simply saying 'Amen', or you could repeat this traditional prayer: 'Lord, have mercy. Christ, have mercy. Lord, have mercy.'

If you can't find stones easily, you might write down the things you want to confess on pieces of paper. If you use thin paper such as kitchen towel, then you can watch it dissolve in the water. Or use normal paper, and when the pieces have soaked in the water for a while, squash them together into a ball.

DOODLE VERSION

If you don't have access either to stones or water, then use the doodle pile of stones provided opposite.

Put your finger on a stone, and just as if you were holding an actual stone, as in the experiment above, name to yourself one thing you want to confess. You could write your confession, in pencil, on the stone, or just say it to yourself. Then colour in the stone as you offer it to God, covering the writing completely – or rub it out. Let each stone become part of a beautiful cairn rather than simply a dead weight in your life.

WHEN I TRIED THIS EXPERIMENT I FOUND . . .

AS I HELD EACH STONE, I FELT . . .

AS I PUT EACH STONE IN THE WATER, I FELT . . .

THE THING I FOUND MOST VALUABLE WAS . . .

THINGS I WOULD TRY CHANGING NEXT TIME:

EXPERIMENT #7

ACTS:

THANKSGIVING

MORE THAN POLITENESS

Do you remember being given something as a child, and having parents or teachers hiss to you 'say thank you!'? You may also be aware of having been the one doing the hissing yourself! Saying please and thank you is a basic element of the politeness that is dinned into us from childhood.

But strangely enough, having learned to be polite can be a problem when it comes to prayers of thankfulness. We don't say thank you to God for quite the same reasons as we thank other people. We don't say thank you to God just to be polite, or to make God feel better. We say thank you to God mainly because of what doing so does to us. Saying thank you means that we are doing two important things:

1 We are choosing to look at the good things in our lives with gratitude, not just focus on the things that aren't right; and

2 We are acknowledging that everything we have comes from God.

That is, first, we are choosing to concentrate on the good. There is an old saying, 'Count your blessings', and it is generally true that if we focus on the good things in life rather than the bad, we are likely to be much happier. Focusing on the positive doesn't mean ignoring the negative aspects of life – after all, sometimes things are seriously wrong and need to be challenged. But even in the worst situations there may be some good for which we can give thanks to God.

Second, when we thank God for all the good things we have received, we are acknowledging that everything comes from God. This has at least two more implications. First, it means we are recognizing God as the Creator, the basic source of everything, from the Big Bang onwards. So thanking God is a statement of faith. Second, it means we are recognizing that all the good things we have are not ours by right, but are gifts. Even the things that we ourselves have achieved or earned are only ours because of the gifts of character, talent and aptitude that we were born with, and the circumstances in which we were born. How much would we have been able to achieve had we been born several hundred years ago, or not had an education?

So thanking God means both recognizing ourselves as gifted people – literally people who have received God's gifts – and at the same time cultivating a sense of humility. In thanking God for our gifts we gradually come to see ourselves as someone whom God loves and showers with gifts, while yet being no more special or loved by God than anyone else.

THE EXPERIMENT

Because it means all this, saying thank you to God is an important part of the Christian tradition of prayer. But it can often become quite repetitive and boring. People often find that when it comes to saying thank you, their mind goes blank! Or we repeat ourselves, saying thank you to God for the same, obvious things every time we pray.

To help focus your prayers of thanksgiving, try making a Jar of Thankfulness.

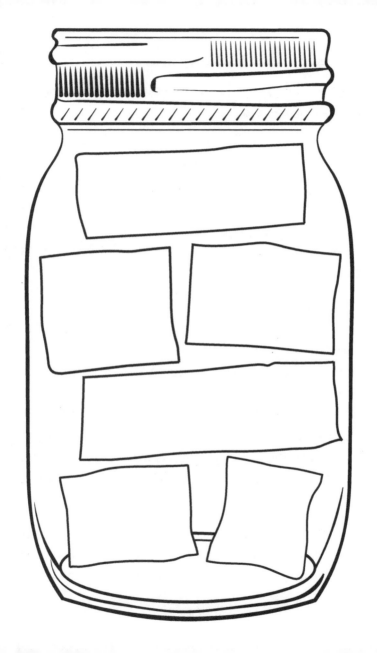

1 Get an empty, clean jar – a jam jar with the label removed would work well.

2 Cut some paper into strips. Coloured paper works well if you're using a glass jar.

3 On each piece of paper, write one thing that you are thankful for, and add the pieces of paper to the jar. Keep a spare supply of pieces of paper next to the jar, and whenever you think of something new to say thanks for, add it to the jar.

Once you have your Jar of Thankfulness, keep it somewhere safe where you will see it regularly – perhaps on a windowsill or your bedside table, or in a prayer corner with any other prayer items that you may have. When you sit down to pray, take out a handful of the contents and say thank you for those, adding to the jar any new ones you have thought of that day. Doing this will mean you keep some variety in your prayers, while also slowly building up a collection of more and more things to be thankful for.

Another idea is to start a jar on New Year's Day (or at another significant date, such as your birthday) each year, and add the good things that happen to you and those that you are thankful for as they happen over the year. Then, on the anniversary of starting the jar (or any time you need a boost), open it up and read all the slips of paper you have collected.

DOODLE VERSION

You can also write, draw or doodle things that you are thankful for on the doodle spaces provided on page 63. You don't have to fill up all the spaces the first time you do this. Try coming back to doodling over a few days, adding one or two new items each time, as well as reading back over those you put down before.

WHEN I TRIED THIS EXPERIMENT I FOUND . . .

AS I ADDED THINGS TO THE JAR I FELT . . .

WHEN I TOOK THINGS OUT OF THE JAR AND PRAYED THEM . . .

THE THING I FOUND MOST VALUABLE WAS . . .

THINGS I WOULD TRY CHANGING NEXT TIME:

EXPERIMENT #8
ACTS:
SUPPLICATION

Supplication (also known as *asking*, or *intercession*) is the final element of ACTS, the four-part balanced diet of prayer. This is probably the kind of prayer that you are most familiar with. Supplication means asking God to do things, to look after others, and to intervene in difficult situations, and for many people this is what praying mainly consists of.

Most church services feature a time of intercessory prayer, during which the concerns of the congregation are lifted up to God. Typically this time will include prayers for the Church, the world, the suffering, and those who have died or are dying and their families. These prayers are often referred to simply as 'The Prayers', when they are in fact just one of the many kinds of prayer that are used in the service.

ASKING GOD FOR WHAT YOU WANT

Sometimes, this kind of praying is criticized or looked down on, as if it was merely about sending a wish list to a kind of cosmic Father Christmas. But although *just* asking God for things would be a very limited kind of praying, asking God is something that Jesus told people to do. Jesus included the line 'give us today our daily bread' in the Lord's Prayer, the prayer he taught his disciples when they asked him to teach them how to pray. Moreover, one of the parables (stories with a message) that Jesus told was the parable of the persistent widow:

'In a certain town there was a judge who neither feared God nor cared what people thought. And there was a widow in that town who kept coming to him with the plea, "Grant me justice against my adversary."

'For some time he refused. But finally he said to himself, "Even though I don't fear God or care what people think, yet because this widow keeps bothering me, I will see that she gets justice, so that she won't eventually come and attack me!"' And the Lord said, 'Listen to what the unjust judge says. And will not God bring about justice for his chosen ones, who cry out to him day and night?' (Luke 18.2–7)

Far from being embarrassed to ask God for the things we need and desire, then, we should make sure we regularly include an element of asking in our prayers. But, as with thanksgiving, asking God to help means a lot more than just what it seems on the surface. In no particular order:

It means admitting that we can't achieve everything we want to happen by ourselves. Very often there are situations around the world, and closer to home, that make us feel helpless. We believe we are incapable of making a difference, and yet we feel very strongly that something must be done. In asking God's help, we are acknowledging the limits of our own influence.

We are also, at the same time, opening ourselves up to the possibility that we may have to do something to be part of the solution. In asking God to help in a particular situation, it is always worth listening for a while afterwards, in case something that you can do occurs to you. In this kind of prayer we consciously volunteer ourselves as God's assistants or co-workers in bringing about change.

Supplication is also a confession of faith in God. By asking God to intervene in a situation, we are saying we believe that God has the power to do so. This doesn't mean we expect miracles to happen every time we pray, but it does mean we are opening our minds to the possibility that God's transforming power will make a difference in the world. Regularly asking for God's help cultivates an attitude of hopeful expectancy in us.

WHAT TO ASK FOR

It is OK to ask for anything that is on your mind! The Bible is full of examples of people asking for what they most want, from good things like food, water or justice to bad things like revenge.

The rule of thumb is to be honest. Tell God what you are really feeling, what you are desperate about, what you want more than anything in the world. The Christian belief is that God knows what you are thinking anyway, of course, so you might as well be honest. God isn't going to think any better of you for trying to hide your true feelings and desires. And you can trust God to know if something you are asking for would be really bad for you or for other people, and to do whatever is most loving.

We know from the Bible that God can intervene in the world to change things, but also that it is quite unusual for miracles to happen. So while it is worth praying for what seems to be the impossible, it's best to be prepared for your prayers to be answered in ways other than those you expected or were hoping for. For example, not everyone who we pray for who is ill will get better: everyone dies at some time. But even then we can trust that God will hear our prayers and help such people to die at peace and be with God in heaven after they die, and comfort those who mourn.

THE EXPERIMENT

To help you think more clearly about what to ask God for and to remember the things that you want to pray for, make a prayer tree.

1 Gather some twigs, and put them in a vase or empty jam jar; or you could use a fairly substantial potted plant, or even a jewellery tree.

2 Now get some little notes to hang on the twigs.
The easiest thing is to use gift tags with a hanging
loop of thread already attached. Or just use
pieces of paper, either plain or cut out to look
like leaves. Use a hole punch or a sharp pencil to
make a hole in each one, and feed through a loop
of thread, wool or gift ribbon so it can be hung on
the tree.

3 Write the name of each person you want to pray for,
or the situation that you want to ask God's help
for, on one of the tags, and hang it on the tree,
consciously giving that person or situation to God
and handing over your worry about it to God as
you do so.

Sit and pray through each of the tags each day, or
once a week, and add new ones whenever you like.
When someone or something no longer needs praying
for, you can remove the tag from the tree. You might
want to keep any prayers that you feel have been
answered in a box: if you keep adding to the tree
regularly, then this box could become a lovely record
of answered prayers.

DOODLE VERSION

You can also use the doodle prayer tree leaves provided on page 75. Write or doodle a person, situation or problem that you want to ask for God's help with on each leaf. You can add new prayer requests to blank leaves over a period of time, or even draw new leaves yourself. And you can add notes to the prayer leaves as the situation changes over time.

WHEN I TRIED THIS EXPERIMENT I FOUND . . .

MAKING THE PRAYER TREE . . .

AS I ADDED PRAYERS TO THE TREE . . .

THE THING I FOUND MOST VALUABLE WAS . . .

THINGS I WOULD TRY CHANGING NEXT TIME:

EXPERIMENT #9

THE LORD'S PRAYER

THE PRAYER THAT JESUS TAUGHT

If you find praying difficult, you might be reassured to know that even the first disciples didn't really know what to do. One of the things they found strangest about Jesus was that he regularly went off on his own to pray (see for example Mark 1.35–37).

The disciples asked Jesus to teach them how to pray, and he taught them the short form of prayer that we now call 'The Lord's Prayer'. There are slightly different versions of it in different accounts (see Matthew 6.9–13 and Luke 11.1–4), and the versions we use today vary slightly between churches, but all are similar.

Our Father in heaven,
hallowed be your name,
your kingdom come,
your will be done,
on earth as in heaven.
Give us today our daily bread,
Forgive us our sins

as we forgive those who sin against us.
Lead us not into temptation
but deliver us from evil.
For the kingdom, the power, and the glory are yours
now and for ever.
Amen.

USING THE LORD'S PRAYER

What is not known is how Jesus meant these words
to be used. Did he mean 'say exactly these words'?
Or did he mean 'include these topics when you pray'?
Or even simply, 'here's an example of the kind of short,
simple way you might go about praying'? We don't
know. But we say the Lord's Prayer in almost every
church service, and many Christians use it every day
as part of their own prayers. It used to be the first
prayer that children were taught, and one of the
things you had to be able to recite to be considered
a Christian.

Simply saying the Lord's Prayer – reciting the familiar
words – is a good way to start or end prayers, and

saying it every day is a good idea. Doing so is very reassuring if you aren't sure what to say, because you know that you are doing what Jesus told his followers to do.

THE EXPERIMENT

One way to use the Lord's Prayer is to think of it as a series of headings, or bullet points, allowing you to make sure that you have covered all the important subjects in your prayers.

Go through it slowly, phrase by phrase. As you do so, spend a minute or two thinking about each phrase and what it means for you, and pray for what it means in your life, or for things you are worried about at the moment. Don't worry if some lines mean more to you than others.

You might want to write the prayer out, very slowly, or rewrite it in your own words, or note down something about what each line means for you personally. You can do so on pages 91–2 of this book.

You could also use the ideas in the chapter 'Colouring the Bible' (pp. 2–8) here, by writing out the Lord's Prayer decoratively, really thinking about what colour, lettering style and illustrations to use for each word or phrase, to reflect their meaning for you.

Here are some ideas about each phrase to start you thinking.

OUR FATHER IN HEAVEN

If God is our father – our creator, and someone who loves and cares for us – what does that mean? And what does it mean for our relationship with other people, if God is their father too? Your relationship with your own parents might influence how this line feels for you. What is it like to try addressing God as 'Mother' or 'Father and Mother', instead of just 'Father'? Why might this feel different?

HALLOWED BE YOUR NAME

This means 'may everyone call you holy'. It's about recognizing that God is totally pure, that God is goodness, truth, light and life. We often talk about a 'holistic' view of life, meaning that everything is held together in one united whole, and 'holy' carries that meaning too. It isn't just any person we call our father, but the God who is utterly holy, who holds all things together, and at the same time is so personal that he loves us and wants us to love him. What does holiness mean to you?

In some religions, the name(s) of God are very important, and in Christianity there is a long tradition of focusing on the name of God. That's why we write it with a capital letter. What names for God are most important to you?

YOUR KINGDOM COME

Much of what Jesus is recorded to have said in the Gospels was about him announcing that God's kingdom both was coming, and had already started (in Jesus himself). What do you hope would be different about life in God's kingdom?

YOUR WILL BE DONE

This part of the prayer says 'I want all the things I am asking for, but I accept it is up to you whether I get them. I believe you know what is best for me and everyone, and I trust you.' It also reminds us of Jesus praying in the Garden of Gethsemane the night before he was killed, accepting whatever God's will for him was (Luke 22.39–46).

ON EARTH AS IN HEAVEN

This means that we don't just aim to get through our present life and look forward to a better life afterwards: we want to work with God to make this world a better place. How might you be called to help that come about?

GIVE US TODAY OUR DAILY BREAD

Here we are asking for what we need, but not for everything we would like: we are only asking for enough to supply our needs today. So we are trusting

God one day at a time, and trying not to worry too much about the future. This can be really difficult, and that's OK. But saying these words reminds us gently to try to worry about just one day at a time.

FORGIVE US OUR SINS

We might not feel we have 'sins', as it sounds quite heavy and serious. But Jesus included these words for everyone. Saying them means we are admitting to God that we are less than perfect. We are both asking God to show us how we could be better people, and trusting that our faults will never stop God loving us and hearing our prayers. We say 'us' and 'our' sins, not 'me' and 'my' sins, because we are also asking for forgiveness for all the things that we as a society get wrong.

AS WE FORGIVE THOSE WHO SIN AGAINST US

People often misunderstand what this means. Forgiving doesn't mean forgetting. For example, you can forgive someone for crashing your car into a bollard without having to let them borrow it again the next day. You can forgive someone who has let you down or hurt you, but you might be sensible to think twice before you trust that person again. I think 'forgiving' means something like 'letting go'. If you are angry with someone, it can feel like letting him or her off if you choose to stop being angry. But Christians believe – and scientists agree – that choosing not to hold on to anger makes you a happier and healthier person.

LEAD US NOT INTO TEMPTATION

This and the next line are both asking for bad things not to happen. 'Temptation' is when we feel we want to do something that we know is wrong. This line asks that we will be protected from finding ourselves in situations where we have to make difficult decisions, or where we are tempted to do something that will hurt ourselves or others. The human brain is very good at justifying to ourselves the things that we want to do – we tell ourselves 'it won't hurt anyone', or 'everyone is doing it'. In the privacy of your own prayers, ask yourself honestly: when are you tempted to do something wrong?

BUT DELIVER US FROM EVIL

This line is a catch-all prayer asking for protection from everything that is bad or frightening. Evil will mean different things to different people: illness, death, people wanting to hurt us. And maybe it is also asking for help for us not to be evil to others?

FOR THE KINGDOM, THE POWER, AND THE GLORY ARE YOURS NOW AND FOR EVER. AMEN

This isn't part of the original prayer that the Bible records Jesus teaching the disciples, but is a way of rounding off the prayer when we use it. It is also a statement of faith that because God is the same for ever, everything that Jesus showed us about God is still true. So we can pray all this trusting that God loves us, and has the power to help us.

'Amen' simply means 'Let it be so'.

Note down beneath these headings what each line of the Lord's Prayer means for you.

OUR FATHER IN HEAVEN,

HALLOWED BE YOUR NAME,

YOUR KINGDOM COME,

YOUR WILL BE DONE,

ON EARTH AS IN HEAVEN.

GIVE US TODAY OUR DAILY BREAD.

FORGIVE US OUR SINS

AS WE FORGIVE THOSE WHO SIN AGAINST US

LEAD US NOT INTO TEMPTATION

BUT DELIVER US FROM EVIL.

FOR THE KINGDOM, THE POWER, AND THE GLORY ARE YOURS
NOW AND FOR EVER. AMEN.

PRAYING LIKE THIS MADE ME FEEL . . .

THE LINE OF THE PRAYER THAT STOOD OUT MOST FOR ME WAS . . .

THE THING I FOUND MOST SURPRISING WAS . . .

THINGS I WOULD TRY CHANGING NEXT TIME:

EXPERIMENT #10
PRAYING WITH YOUR BODY

THE MIND/BODY CONNECTION

How much do you think about what you do with your body when you pray? Scientists are continually finding more connections between our bodies and our minds. We are not just a mind in a body, like a computer in a case. Our bodies are part of us, and what we do with our bodies can shape our thinking.

Try this: smile. You actually feel happier when you make the muscle movements that form a smile, even if you are only acting.

We don't tend to think much about what we do with our bodies when we are praying, though you might well remember being told as a child to pray 'Hands together, eyes closed'. The idea of that was simply to stop you being distracted. In some churches, you will find that people stand, sit and kneel at different parts of the service. It can be confusing if you go to a church you aren't used to, as not all churches choose the same posture for the same bits!

PRAYER POSITIONS

How many different physical ways of praying can you think of?

Originally, in Roman times, people seem to have stood to pray, with their arms outstretched. In many churches, the posture of the priest during the communion prayer is a descendant of this.

Kneeling became fashionable in the Middle Ages. It was a position that people were used to because you knelt before your lord, or the king. Kneeling was used because as people began to develop a more personal idea of God, they related to God as they would to their social superior. A similar theme can be seen in other cultures. Muslims, for example, bow, kneel, and then bow their heads to the ground in prayer, which again imitates the kind of posture used in the presence of a king or superior in Eastern medieval culture.

In some times and places, people lie face down on the floor to pray. This is called prostration, and it is usually kept for particularly serious times of prayer. In the past, monks or nuns might pray all night lying on the floor before taking vows to join a monastery, and a knight might do the same before a battle. In some churches today the posture is used on Good Friday, or at the ordination of new clergy.

Nowadays, the most common posture for prayer is sitting down. Differences are mostly about what you do with your hands. Are they to be clasped together? Flat together? Open on your knees, as if you are waiting to receive something from God? In the air, as if you are carried away at a rock concert or celebrating a goal?

THE EXPERIMENT

In this experiment, you can try out several different postures for prayer, and see how they make you feel about the relationship between you and God.

1 Find somewhere you know you won't be disturbed, so you don't feel embarrassed at being found in a

variety of strange positions! Then try standing, with your arms out (like a priest at the altar). Imagine you are standing before God. How does it feel to be in front of God like this?

2 Next, kneel down, either on one or both knees. This is rather like kneeling before the monarch to be knighted; or pleading with a lord for some favour, or for mercy. Imagine you are kneeling in front of God: how does it feel?

3 Now lie down, flat on your front. Legs together, arms outstretched – a bit like a lying down crucifix. Are you lying in front of God? How does that feel? Or are you imagining what it was like to be Christ on the cross?

4 Now sit on a chair. Imagine Jesus pulling up a chair and sitting next to you. How does it feel to be talking to God in this position? Try some different positions for your hands too.

5 If your body comes up with other positions, then give those a try. Think about how each position makes you feel, both in yourself and in relation to God, if you imagine God there in the room with you.

WHEN I TRIED THIS EXPERIMENT I FOUND . . .

STANDING MADE ME FEEL . . .

KNEELING MADE ME FEEL . . .

LYING DOWN MADE ME FEEL . . .

SITTING MADE ME FEEL . . .

THE THING I FOUND MOST VALUABLE OR
SURPRISING WAS . . .

THINGS I WOULD TRY CHANGING NEXT TIME:

EXPERIMENT #11
PRAYING WITH BEADS

PRAYING WITH BEADS

Using beads to help you pray has a long history. The most commonly known example is the rosary, which is especially popular in Roman Catholic devotion as an aid to a set of prayers focusing on Mary, the mother of Jesus. The traditional rosary has five sets of ten small beads, with each set separated by a single larger bead. The Lord's Prayer is said at the beginning of each set, then a short prayer to Mary is said ten times, while at the same time the person praying thinks about a particular prayer topic or 'mystery'. The rosary is a development of much older prayer aids using knotted string or rope, the prayers being said as your fingers pass along each knot.

Praying like this is quite different from most modern forms of prayer, which emphasize a personal conversation with God. Instead, these historic forms of prayer focus on simply reciting set prayers a number of times. This idea has sometimes been criticized for being empty or superstitious, but many people find that using such a prayer method helps them to focus on God – rather like the meditation techniques discussed on pages 22–7.

The idea is usually threefold. Put very simply, it works as follows:

1 Each bead, or knot, reminds you to pray for something.

2 Your hands and mind are kept busy by touching the beads, so you are less likely to be distracted by other things.

3 The physical action of taking up the beads and going through them one by one makes you take time out to pray.

The picture on page 107 is of a modern example of prayer beads, the 'Pearls of Life'. These were invented in 1995 by Swedish bishop Martin Lonnebo, who was trying to come up with a modern version of prayer beads that helped people to think not just about Mary, but about their relationship with God. If you want to read more, his book *Pearls of Life: For the Personal Spiritual Journey* (Wild Goose Publications, 2007) explains how he came to invent them, and how to use them. Although you can buy the beads ready made to go with the book, if you wish, I think it makes them much more personal and meaningful if you make a set yourself – and making them helps you remember the meaning of each bead, too.

THE EXPERIMENT

The exercise involves first making your own prayer bracelet, and then wearing it and using it.

First, you will need a stock of beads (or buttons would do), and a piece of string, wool or elastic. The picture on page 107 shows the original 'Pearls of Life' layout:

you can copy this, or you could make a simpler version of your own. The suggested sizes and colours given here will help you remember what the beads each represent, but you could choose whatever sizes and colours you like, or whatever is available easily.

1 Tie a knot in the string to stop the beads slipping off. Then choose a large gold bead (or another one that seems special to you), and start by putting this on the string. This is the God bead.

2 Find six similar plain beads – in the picture they are long and wooden. These are used to create space between the special beads, and are called the beads of Silence, or peace. Put one on next, and set the others aside to use later on.

3 The third bead represents you. Try to find a small pearl-like bead, or another one that you feel characterizes you better.

4 A large white bead comes next: this one represents your baptism, becoming and being a member of the Church.

5 Put another Silence bead on, then a bigger, sandy-coloured, maybe rough-textured bead. This is the Desert bead, and represents the rough and bleak parts of your life.

6 Another Silence bead, then a big blue bead: this is called the Carefree bead. It might remind you of the sky or the sea. This one represents being happy and relaxed, and trusting God.

7 Add another Silence bead, and then two big red beads. These represent God's love for us in the birth of Jesus, and in Jesus' death for us – the incarnation and the crucifixion.

8 Then come three small Mystery beads. They might be pearls, or silver, or whatever you like. These are for whoever or whatever you feel it is most important to pray for and about. You could choose one bead to represent each thing or person, or each one might hold a whole group of concerns. For example, one could stand for your family, one for friends, one for issues that you are worrying about.

9 Next, add a big black bead to represent Night, death and darkness.

10 Add another Silence bead, and then a big white bead for Resurrection, finishing with the last Silence bead.

Make your bracelet following this pattern, and then either wear it as a constant reminder of prayer, or just pick it up and use it when you pray.

There aren't any particular prayers to use, but if you want more reflection on the different beads you could try googling 'Pearls of Life', or reading Bishop Lonnebo's book, to find prayers or meditations written about each bead. But the main way of using the beads is simply to go through them one by one.

Touch the first bead with your fingers: hold it between finger and thumb. Think about what it means and then think about what that means to you, today. Then move on to the next one. Remember what it represents: think about it for a few seconds, or a few minutes. When you reach a Silence bead, sit in silence for a minute or two. And so on, all round the bracelet.

PRAYING WITH BEADS

Most people find that the first few times they use their beads, they need to refer back to the instructions to remember what each bead stands for; but soon the meanings become familiar enough to remember. You might like to wear the beads as a bracelet, so that you are reminded of God whenever you see them. People have commented that you can use them to pray whenever you have a spare moment while you are out and about, without anyone even noticing what you are doing.

DOODLE VERSION

If you can't easily find beads, then try doodling on page 113.

Choosing what you'd like each 'bead' to represent, colour or decorate each one. Then use it by letting your finger rest on each bead around the circle, thinking about what it represents, just as if you had a real bracelet. You could also label each bead with its meaning, and jot down or doodle the thoughts, prayers and ideas that come to you as pray with the page.

WHEN I TRIED THIS EXPERIMENT I FOUND . . .

AS I WAS MAKING THE BRACELET . . .

PRAYING WITH THE BEADS FELT . . .

THE THING I FOUND MOST VALUABLE WAS . .

THINGS I WOULD TRY CHANGING NEXT TIME:

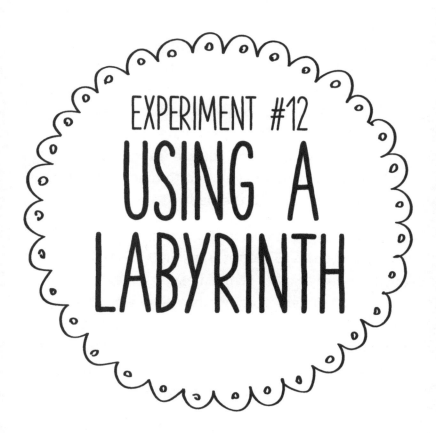

EXPERIMENT #12
USING A LABYRINTH

WHAT IS A LABYRINTH?

A labyrinth looks like a flat maze, with a way in and out and a path to the centre. But a labyrinth differs from a maze in that it only has one path. The path winds round and back on itself, so you can seem suddenly very near the centre, then very far away. There are various different designs, some more complex than others, but whichever one you are using you know you can't get lost. All you have to do to reach the centre is simply keep following the path.

Labyrinths are normally circular, and can be very big – as much as 15 metres in diameter. Full-size labyrinths like this are sometimes set in stone into church floors (there is a famous example at Chartres Cathedral in France), and are sometimes laid out in gardens in turf or as brick paths. Smaller versions can be drawn on a handkerchief and kept in your pocket, or printed on paper or a tile, or carved into wood.

Labyrinths have been used since ancient times as symbols of the spiritual life, and since at least medieval times as symbols of the Christian path. They were used

as an alternative to costly and impractical pilgrimages for people who couldn't easily travel. The journey to the middle of the labyrinth might represent travelling to Jerusalem, or meeting God face to face, or reaching the end of life.

USING LABYRINTHS

There are various ways to use a labyrinth, but the pure method, with a full-size labyrinth, is simply to slowly follow the path to the centre, rest there a while, and then slowly follow it back out. It is a method of praying using your whole body. You don't merely sit still and think, your body actually makes a journey. In my experience of walking full-size labyrinths, I have found that my mind follows that physical journey, and is able to make connections that I'm not sure I'd have made if I were just sitting still.

An alternative is to use the labyrinth by thinking about a particular question, or reflecting on a particular issue, as you walk. Some people read a scriptural quotation on the way in, and perhaps another on the way out. Some might deliberately think about their own journey through life as they walk.

THE EXPERIMENT

First, find your labyrinth. Full-size labyrinths are big, and expensive and time-consuming to build, but if there is one near you then do give walking it a try. I have an oak finger labyrinth, about 18 inches across with a grooved path carved into the wood: you might be able to find one of these to borrow. Most easily, you can print out a simple labyrinth pattern from the internet (just look up 'labyrinth pattern'), or use the small one on page 123.

Once you have your labyrinth, it is time to 'walk' it. All you have to do is trace the path, either with your finger or with a pen. Try to go as slowly as possible. Notice how you feel. Do you have to resist the urge to go faster? Do you find any parts of the path more frustrating, or annoying, or fun, than others? When you get to the middle, stop for a while. How does it feel to be there? How do you feel about following the path back out again? When you are ready, follow the path out, again noticing how you feel.

You can either just trace the path and see where your thoughts take you, or you might prefer to focus on a set of words. Why not follow the labyrinth twice, and give both a try?

When you use words, I suggest the first time thinking about two things that Jesus said about being a path for us to follow. You could think on the way in about Jesus saying 'I am the way, the truth and the life'; and on the way out about the words 'Follow me'. Or, if there is a particular matter that is bothering you, try asking

USING A LABYRINTH

God to help you think about it as you follow the path, and see what happens.

DOODLE VERSION

If you have printed out a paper labyrinth, or are using the one reproduced opposite. You could use pens or pencils of different colours to trace the path in and out. Note down any ideas and thoughts that occur to you as you go around the path, either in the space at the corners of the page or along the path itself. You could also trace the pattern on to cloth and use fabric pens to make it permanent, or even try drawing a bigger version yourself using the one illustrated here as a guide.

'WALKING' AROUND THE LABYRINTH MADE ME FEEL . . .

ON THE WAY OUT AGAIN . . .

THE THING I FOUND MOST VALUABLE WAS . . .

THINGS I WOULD TRY CHANGING NEXT TIME:

EXPERIMENT #13
DOOR PRAYERS

MAKING AN ENTRANCE

What is the front door of your house like? Do you decorate it on special occasions? Balloons tied to a door or gatepost before a party tell people to expect fun inside; a Christmas wreath on the door makes the house feel festive and welcoming. You might have pots of flowers at the entrance to your house, or a 'Welcome' door mat. What we put at entrances sets an atmosphere.

In many religious traditions, written prayers or short blessings are placed on doorways. As well as asking God to bless the house or room, the idea is that every time you enter or leave the house, you are reminded to pray. You don't even have to consciously say the prayer each time, you just see it and notice it as you are passing.

THE EXPERIMENT

Try writing doorway prayers for your house.

1 First, think about the entrance to your house: your front door, or hallway or porch. What would you like

a prayer or blessing that you see going into or out of the house to say?

Perhaps: 'God bless this house'.

Or: 'God, be with me in this place'.

Or: 'Peace be in this house'.

Or you might want to choose a Bible verse, perhaps the first verse of Psalm 67: 'May God be gracious to us and bless us and make his face shine on us.' Or this, from Matthew's Gospel: 'Everyone then who hears these words of mine and acts on them will be like a wise man who built his house on rock' (Matthew 7.24, NRSV).

You could choose one of those, or write your own.

2 You can also make a sign for a particular room. Think about what you might be doing as you enter or leave the room, and what you might need a prayer for. For example, if the room is your bedroom, you might be going in to go to bed, or you might just be popping in to get a jumper or collect the washing; or you might be leaving in the morning facing a difficult situation at work, or going to bed worried

about what the day has held. If you choose the kitchen, you might be going in to cook a meal or do some chores, or perhaps to sit and read the paper; it might be a place that you find peaceful and creative, or it might be a place of stress and anxiety for you.

You might write a prayer sign saying 'God bless all my thoughts and dreams'.

Or: 'God grant me patience and peace'.

Or: 'God, protect and surround me with your love'.

Or: 'Bless and protect all who gather here'...

Or something else?

3 When you've decided what to put on each sign, write or print them out. Mount the signs on a piece of paper or card, and decorate them as much as you like. Make them something you will enjoy seeing. You could even try knitting or embroidering them. Make sure the writing is big enough for you to be able to read it as you approach the door. Then stick each sign up by the doorway you have chosen, where you will see it every time you go in or out.

4 Leave the signs there for at least a week. For the first day or two, deliberately say the prayers – either out loud, or quietly to yourself – every time you see them. After that, you will probably find you hear them in your head anyway, but make sure you notice them each time you go in or out.

If you like this idea, what other doors might you make prayer signs for?

WHEN I TRIED THIS EXPERIMENT I FOUND . . .

MAKING THE SIGNS MADE ME FEEL . . .

AS I WENT PAST THEM . . .

THE THING I FOUND MOST VALUABLE WAS . . .

THINGS I WOULD TRY CHANGING NEXT TIME:

EXPERIMENT #14
EXAMEN

PRAYING THROUGH YOUR DAY

Do you sometimes feel stuck for what to pray about? Sometimes we can get into a rut, or feel that there is nothing in particular to pray about today. One way of avoiding this situation is to use the Christian tradition of the 'Examen'. This is a structured way of reflecting, through prayer, on the last 24 hours of your life, which means you never have to worry about finding something to pray for or about! Everyone always has the past day to reflect on.

The idea is to walk through your day in your memory, noticing moments when you felt any particularly strong emotions or feelings – whether positive or negative – and identifying any incidents or encounters that seem to stick in your mind, or to leap out at you as you recall the day's events. If something jumps out at you, or is associated with strong emotions, it is worth thinking about more closely.

WHY DO THIS?

Spending some time at the end of the day
examining what has gone on is an old Christian
tradition, particularly associated with St Ignatius.
It was advocated by some Greek philosophers
before Christianity too. Often called the 'Examination
of Conscience', it is the traditional way in which Roman
Catholics were taught to prepare for confession to a
priest: go through everything you can remember doing,
and examine carefully what your motivations were. In
the past, the emphasis was very much on looking for
sins, but the modern approach to the Examen is to
focus on closely examining your consciousness, and
especially your feelings and emotions.

The idea is that God can be found in our everyday
lives. By ensuring that we pay attention in prayer to
the detail of our day-to-day activities – the trip to work,
an argument on the bus, someone you met, a moment
when you felt surprising anger, joy, fear or excitement –
the Examen helps us to get used to seeing all of life
as a place where God meets with us. The incarnation –
God being born as a human at Christmas – is a sign

of this. So too are the sacraments of the Church, like Holy Communion or Baptism: moments when God is encountered in everyday things, like bread, wine and water.

The Examen also helps you to take your own emotions and feelings seriously. Reflecting on them helps you to develop a reflective wisdom about yourself. If you make a habit of it, you will find that you gradually become less swept away by strong feelings; you will develop the wisdom to examine them, see what is really going on, and come to understand what your emotions are signalling to you.

THE EXPERIMENT

There are six steps to the Examen.

1 Start with a short prayer for understanding or light. Pray that God will shine a torch on the things you should be concentrating on as you go through the day.

2 Then begin by looking for good things, things to be thankful for. Go back over the past 24 hours noticing anything that was good, enjoyable, or seemed especially meaningful. It could be a flower in the wall

that you noticed as you passed, a conversation that struck you, time with a friend. Say thank you to God for whatever occurs to you.

3 Now imagine yourself walking through the day once again. Follow yourself in your imagination: where did you go, who did you see? Notice the feelings – positive and negative – that rise up as you remember the day, and observe any incidents that jump out at you.

4 Choose one of these incidents to focus on, the one that is associated with the strongest feelings. It doesn't matter if the feeling is positive or negative – that will vary from day to day. Trust that what jumps out at you is the thing God wants you to examine more closely, even if it seems trivial or painful. The fact that it has jumped out at you is the result of the prayer for enlightenment that you began with.

Now imagine picking up that incident and turning it around in the air, looking carefully at it – like a jeweller examining all the different facets of a diamond. Think about what was really going on. What led up to the incident? Why did you react the way you did? What were your real motivations for what you did or said? How does looking at it now make you feel?

Ask God if there is anything else you should notice about it.

Pray for anything that has arisen out of your examination.

If there were two or three things that jumped out at you as you reviewed the day, you might want to carry out the same process again for each of them.

5 Next, think briefly about the day to come. Mentally walk through what you are expecting to happen: your diary entries, any encounters or activities you are looking forward to or are concerned about. Again, note what your feelings or emotions are as you imagine going through tomorrow. Pray about anything that arises.

6 Finally, imagine handing over to God everything you have thought about. You could imagine literally gathering each item up and putting them at the foot of the cross: things you are grateful for, things you are worried about, whatever your thoughts have led you to. End by saying the Lord's Prayer.

WHEN I TRIED THIS EXPERIMENT I FOUND . . .

AS I WENT BACK OVER THE DAY . . .

AS I THOUGHT ABOUT TOMORROW . . .

THE THING I FOUND MOST VALUABLE OR
SURPRISING WAS . . .

THINGS I WOULD TRY CHANGING NEXT TIME:

Did you know that SPCK is a registered charity?

As well as publishing great books by leading Christian authors, we also . . .

. . . **make assemblies meaningful and fun for over a million children** by running www.assemblies.org.uk, a popular website that provides free assembly scripts for teachers. For many children, school assembly is the only contact they have with Christian faith and culture, and the only time in their week for spiritual reflection.

. . . **help prisoners to become confident readers** with our easy-to-read stories. Poor literacy is a huge barrier to rehabilitation. Prisoners identify with the believable heroes of our gritty fiction. At the same time, questions at the end of each chapter help them to examine their choices from a moral perspective and to build their reading confidence.

. . . **support student ministers overseas in their training**. We give them free, specially written theology books, the International Study Guides. These books really do make a difference, not just to students but to ministers and, through them, to a whole community.

Please support these great schemes: visit www.spck.org.uk/support-us to find out more.